AMERICA'S MOST HAUNTED PLACES

OTHER BOOKS BY NANCY ROBERTS

Animal Ghost Stories

Blackbeard and Other Pirates of the Atlantic Coast

Civil War Ghost Stories and Legends

Ghosts and Specters of the Old South

Ghosts of the Carolinas

Ghosts of the Southern Mountains and Appalachia

Gold Seekers
Gold, Ghosts and Legends from Carolina to California

Haunted Houses
Chilling Tales from American Homes, Second Edition

The Haunted South
Where Ghosts Still Roam

North Carolina Ghosts and Legends

South Carolina Ghosts
From the Coast to the Mountains

Southern Ghosts

America's Most
HAUNTED
PLACES

by

Nancy Roberts

SANDLAPPER PUBLISHING CO., INC.
ORANGEBURG, SOUTH CAROLINA

AMERICA'S MOST HAUNTED PLACES

Library of Congress Cataloging-in-Publication Data

Roberts, Nancy, 1924–
    America's most haunted places.

    Rev. ed. of: America's most haunted places /
Bruce Roberts. 1st ed. 1976.
    Summary: Fifteen ghost stories associated with
historically important locations in the United States
including Fort Ticonderoga, Gettysburg, Harper's Ferry,
and the Comstock Lode.
    1. Ghosts—United States—Juvenile literature.
[1. Ghosts] I. Roberts, Bruce, 1930–
America's most haunted places. II. Title.
BF1472.U6R6 1987   133.1'0973   86-22577
ISBN 0-87844-074-7 (soft)

Contents

AMERICA'S MOST HAUNTED PLACES

The King's Messengers

Riding down the road on a rainy October night, their coats flying out behind them in the wind, come two horsemen. As a car approaches, the riders signal for it to stop.

"Which way to Charlottesburg?" shouts one of them. The driver of the car begins to give directions, but before the words have left his lips, the two men ride off into the night. Who are they and where do they come from? Why do they ask everyone they meet the same question?

Motorists who have seen their faces have hurried on for they say the faces are too horrifying to describe and are the faces of men long dead. Year after year this dreadful pair comes riding, riding out of the past, out of the world of the dead. They come with a message to deliver.

Listen to their story, and when you meet them some rainy October night, you will know why they still ride. You may even have a chance to talk with them if you are not afraid.

During the Revolution an English officer named Major Ferguson waited at a place called King's Mountain where he expected the Americans to attack. He thought he would be able to defeat them, but just to be sure, he

This dreadful pair comes riding.

sent some of his best riders as messengers to Lord Cornwallis to ask for more British soldiers to help him.

But Ferguson received no answer from Cornwallis. Finally he hit upon the idea of sending two farmers from the area who knew the countryside well and were loyal to the British. The farmers, James and Douglas Duncan, thought that the British were going to win the war and they could be sure of keeping their farms, and being rewarded with gold as well, if they helped the British soldiers. They cared little which side won as long as they came out on top.

Early one October evening Ferguson called them to his tent and gave them an envelope directing them to give

10

it to Lord Cornwallis in person. Cornwallis was at Charlottesburg and both men knew the road well. The major told them not to talk to anyone along the way for they were bearing a most important message.

The two brothers galloped along in the dark toward the Catawba River. They knew that on the other side was a fine tavern and they planned to stop there and refresh themselves.

The husband of the poor woman who owned the tavern had been killed by the British at the battle of Camden, South Carolina. The two farmers pretended to be very sorry about this. When they told her what a shame it was for such a fine man to be killed, she gave them an extra measure of whiskey.

The more they drank the looser their tongues became and soon they were bragging about "an important message they must deliver." When the lady began to see that the pair she was treating so kindly were really on an errand for the enemy, her hatred for the British boiled within her. As they prepared to leave she slipped upstairs and stood by the window holding two pistols as she waited for them to pass beneath her. When they appeared she fired first at the man on the right and then at the man on the left. One fell forward a bit but straightened up. The other seemed to jerk in his saddle but neither man fell and the horses dashed off down the muddy road into the night.

Near Salisbury, North Carolina, it was long after midnight when an innkeeper named Amos Bissell heard a pounding at his door. He could not see well outside but he could hear rough, angry voices raised in argument.

"No, we must go back, you simpleton. We have taken

a wrong turn."

"If you know everything why didn't you tell me to take the turn toward the east? That varmint of a woman led us out of our way."

The men continued to argue, each blaming the other and becoming more and more angry. Bissell was afraid their loud voices would awaken his sleeping guests, but no one stirred. Taking his pistol he flattened himself near the crack of the tavern door and peered out.

A map was spread upon the stump of a tree and two men were bending over it. Now they seemed to reach a decision and as they turned he could see their faces illuminated in the moonlight. He would never forget the sight. Their mouths hung open, their eyes stared upward and their flesh was a greenish white. He knew without a doubt that the men were dead. Amos Bissell was so frightened his shaking fingers could scarcely latch the door.

The message from Major Ferguson was never delivered and the Americans won a stunning victory at King's Mountain. Sometime after that, travelers began to report encounters with two horsemen who hailed them and asked the way to Charlottesburg. Those who take the back roads between these two places say that you can see the riders still, particularly if the weather is just right. On and on they ride in the night, trying to deliver a message to a man dead long ago.

The Ghost of Fort Ticonderoga

Great, brooding walls of native stone ringed by cannon look out upon magnificent scenery in every direction. Fort Ticonderoga is almost surrounded by the blue waters of Lake Champlain, and to the south looms the crest of Mount Defiance. Ticonderoga is an impressive fort and it is the last one still commanded by a Revolutionary War general—a general who has never really left, *for the fort is haunted.*

It is haunted by the ghost of the man who once commanded it for the Americans—the ghost of General "Mad Anthony" Wayne. Wayne still occupies his old quarters where he is sometimes glimpsed seated at a table in front of the fire, but most often while he walks the ramparts of the fort inspecting the sentries or watching for a British attack.

Inside the fort are maps, guns, furniture, and uniforms. They date back to the days when French General Montcalm with a handful of men held off the British Army, and a flamboyant Ethan Allen and an ambitious Benedict Arnold seized the fort for the American cause. There is no place in America where the Revolution seems so recent as it does here, and it is still *home* to the ghost of Brigadier General Anthony Wayne.

On one occasion a stone mason was called to the fort in the winter to repair some stones that had been broken in a storm. Dawn comes late in December and in the early morning mist the stone mason looked up to see a figure pacing along the rampart facing Mount Defiance. At first he thought this must be the winter caretaker. He approached the man and was surprised to see that he was wearing a long blue cape and a magnificent blue and white uniform. As the stone mason drew nearer, the man pointed to Mount Defiance and said, "I told them to guard the top of that mountain, but St. Claire gave up my fort without a fight." He did not seem to be speaking to anyone in particular or aware of the stone mason's presence.

Then the tall man in the blue cape turned and walked down the stone steps where he sprang upon the back of the most beautiful horse the mason had ever seen. Faintly, carried by the morning breeze, came the words "On to Stony Point!" And horse and rider were soon out of sight.

Fort Ticonderoga is not the only place where the ghost of Anthony Wayne may be seen. He is a ghost for all seasons. When the warm July winds blow down the Hudson River Valley, his ghost has been seen galloping along the road to Stony Point, the hoofs of the horse striking sparks as they hit the rocks. As the leaves turn in the fall, a phantom horse and rider splash up the Brandywine. And when the snow begins to fall, that same horse and rider have appeared on the hillside at Valley Forge riding among the reconstructed huts once occupied by Wayne's Pennsylvanians. As spring comes, the pair is more often

Great, brooding walls of native stone.

He saw a figure pacing along the rampart facing Mount Defiance.

seen near Lake Champlain.

Anthony Wayne is as resourceful as a ghost as he was as a Revolutionary general, constantly popping up in unexpected places. His horse, Nab, is always with him. If, along the shores of the Hudson, they stop for a moment and the general dismounts to look, Nab will not be far away. Occasionally, campers near Fort Ticonderoga will see him. One campground owner is not surprised when an occasional camper comes to him and tells of having seen the horse and rider. But he always assures them they haven't seen a ghost, they have seen what few people have seen, the American Spirit—full of reckless abandon as if horse and rider were one, confident, exuberant, restless, always moving.

16

There is a tradition of long standing that when General Washington first told Anthony Wayne of his plan to storm Stony Point, Washington looked at him and awaited his reaction. Wayne replied, "General, if you will only plan it, I'll storm hell." Said Washington, "Perhaps, General Wayne, we had better try Stony Point first."

And, so, with his trusted commander gone, General Wayne's ghost doesn't have the plans to storm hell or heaven but is forever destined to ride the road to Stony Point and Ticonderoga, then up the Brandywine to Val-

His ghost has been seen galloping along.

ley Forge. A ghost without a commander-in-chief and without an Army, he still does one thing—in the morning mist at Ticonderoga on the ramparts of the old stone fort, he is still commandant of the fort that once protected America.

The Ghost Hand of Skene Manor

Some of us are afraid of our shadow. Others are not afraid of anything. It is hard to know which sort we are until something happens.

Frightening things should occur only at night when it is dark and rainy. But sometimes they get out of place and that is what happened one summer afternoon in a little town in northern New York.

When we drove into Whitehall the sun shone on the quaint old store fronts and sparkled on the river that divided the middle of the business section. We were looking for a place to have lunch when we saw an impressive black sign with gold letters. The sign read SKENE MANOR, DISTINCTIVE FOOD, and an arrow pointed up a narrow road to our right. *What odd things happen when we turn off a main road—things that can make even a sunny day scary!*

A steep, narrow road led up the side of the mountain to an old home. Grim and foreboding, it most closely resembled a towering, gray stone castle. For a moment we were tempted to leave. Instead we parked the car, climbed the stone steps to an imposing door, and entered an enor-

19

mous hall. The walls were papered with scenes of the past showing life-size people in colonial costumes. We were greeted by the proprietor of this unusual restaurant.

"The tables are not ready yet. Would you like to sit at the bar for a few minutes while you wait?" The bar was a horseshoe of dark, polished wood and behind it were all the usual glasses and bottles. Sipping a glass of wine we stared around us at the handsome carving and mahogany panels that decorated the room. This had been an unusually fine home but there was something weird about it, and, half in fun, I remarked to the owner, "You don't happen to have a ghost here, do you?" He returned my smile but did not reply.

Part of the barroom atmosphere was the pleasant, restful sound of water tumbling from a small fountain behind the bar. *But the sight in the center of the fountain was not so pleasant.* Rising in the midst of the water was the lovely white hand of a woman! On the hand was a beautiful ring. What a strange, macabre jest! Its appearance was a shock, for it was at once white and still and yet so lifelike.

All hunger left me at the sight of this hand, raised as if to plead, and I was ready to suggest that we wait no longer. But before I could do so, our host reappeared and announced that the tables were ready. We entered the dining room and seated ourselves near an Italian marble fireplace. My chair faced the entrance to the dark and cavernous hall. The shutters were closed and the antique lighting fixtures made it seem more like late afternoon than midday. The menu was inviting and I banished uneasy thoughts from my mind.

20

The food was excellent and it was not until the meal was almost over that I began to feel someone was watching us. I glanced toward the hallway but it was empty. A few minutes later I was certain that someone was standing in the doorway. I looked up quickly and saw a woman with a full-skirted dress, her hand resting on the molding. It was a very lovely hand and on the middle finger glinted a large and tantalizingly familiar ring. To my horror I rec-

That is what happened one summer afternoon.

It most closely resembled a towering, gray stone castle.

ognized the ring. It was the same one I had seen on the hand in the fountain!

Before I could reach the doorway the hand had vanished. I was sure I would see its owner when I entered the hall and my heart pounded with excitement. Instead, I found the hall empty.

Then came a sound so faint I was not certain I had heard anything. Was it the click of a doorknob turning? I hurried to the end of the hall and was just in time to see a glowing spot of light take shape. There were the fingers and then the ring, and the hand was turning the knob of the door ever so slightly. I was fascinated by the sparkling ring, and as I stared, the hand became that of a skeleton! The door slammed sharply, and had I not been standing as if in a trance, I would have pulled it open and dashed through in pursuit of that hand—*and whatever it was attached to.* But by the time I was able to move, there was nothing to be seen in the room beyond.

When I returned to the table, my husband was reading the back of the menu.

"Did you know they once had a ghost here?" he asked, smiling. I tried to answer calmly.

"What kind of a ghost?"

Rising in the midst of the water was the lovely white hand of a woman.

23

"The ghost of a lovely lady. The coffin of Colonel Skene's wife was kept in the basement here for a while. Then when this house was first made into a restaurant the owner at that time placed it in a corner of the bar and built a stone fountain around it."

"I can't believe it. A fountain built around a coffin?"

"Yes, and she probably haunts this place. It seems the Colonel was only to keep this property as long as Mrs. Skene remained above ground. He had a lead-lined coffin constructed and placed the body of his wife inside. Do you want to look around? You might see her ghost."

"You would never believe me," I replied.

The Ghost of Gettysburg

(from the Diary of a Union Officer)

Colonel John Pittenger of the Union Army had been sent on one of the most unusual missions of the Civil War. He was trying to find out about a ghost that had been seen by hundreds of men. Something like that should be easy to find out about, but so far it was not, and Pittenger was becoming discouraged.

Each time he saw the curling smoke of a Union campfire, he would hope to find the men of the 20th Maine. They alone could tell him what had really happened. *Was it true that they had seen a ghost at the battle of Gettysburg? And, would they admit it if they had?*

One rainy evening in late July of 1863 he found the camp he had been looking for and asked to speak to the commanding officer. As he and General Oliver J. Hunt sat together in the general's tent, Pittenger thought of many questions he wanted to ask.

"General, you and I both know that war does strange things to the minds of men. Have you heard the story that a colonial officer appeared among our troops at Gettysburg?"

The general stared at him for a moment but did not answer.

"Sir, I realize what an incredible question you probably think that is, and I hope you don't think I am trying to spread foolish talk."

"Colonel Pittenger, I have very little time to waste. I would like to hear your answers to two questions. Is your interest a serious one, and may I count on you not to treat this

It is a terrible thing to watch your men shot to pieces by the enemy.

matter lightly where my men are within earshot?"

Surprised by the general's bluntness, Colonel Pittenger replied that he had been requested to conduct this investigation by Edwin Stanton, Secretary of War under President Lincoln. General Hunt seemed reassured. His brusque manner became friendly and he brought out two glasses and a bottle of sherry wine.

"Colonel, I hope you will forgive me. The last few weeks have been hard on all of us. It is a terrible thing to watch your men shot to pieces by the enemy, but that is what I saw for a long time there at Gettysburg.

"Our lines began to break before the overwhelming number of Rebel soldiers. Our men left their guns. The wounded limped or crawled past me to the rear. In a matter of minutes there was nothing between us and thousands of fiercely yelling Rebel soldiers. It was like the opening

Out of nowhere rode a tall figure on a shining white horse.

of the gates of hell. Our guns let loose but the enemy kept coming through what seemed to be a solid sheet of fire. We had to defend that hill. To lose Little Roundtop would have been to lose everything, but such desperate fighting could not go on for long.

"The shouts and noise of the battle became a roar. Then a terrible thing happened. We ran out of ammunition! I thought we would have to fall back, when out of nowhere rode a tall figure on a shining white horse. I know this is incredible, but the rider was dressed like a Revolutionary general. And the face—I swear to my dying day—it was the face of George Washington! He raised his arm high and gave the signal to advance. My men began to shout and cheer. The Rebels saw it too for they began to shoot at it. The figure rode back and forth and the Confederate guns followed him. He should have been killed a thousand times over. No human being could have survived that fire.

"The rider urged our men on, and raising their bayonets they charged down the hill on top of the Rebels. The bayonet charge must have taken the Rebels by surprise for they turned and fled.

"We almost lost Little Roundtop, Colonel, and if we had we could have lost Gettysburg. You may say what you please, but there is many a man in the 20th Maine who will go to his grave believing that General Washington himself helped save the day.

"And as for my personal feelings, I think Lee would have been in Washington tonight and the war over, except for the apparition. You may tell Secretary Stanton that he was saved by a ghost."

*Those who were
there at the battle
know who haunts
the field at
Gettysburg.*

"This will make an unusual report to the War Department, General."

"I don't expect the War Department to understand anything about it," replied the general. The two men exchanged a long look and shook hands, and Colonel Pittenger left.

There are many who live near Gettysburg today who claim that strange things happen there during the hot summer nights. That a rider on a magnificent white stallion gallops across the battlefield surrounded by a luminous aura. Both horseman and mount gleam in the moonlight and the horse's hoofs strike sparks wherever they touch.

Some say he wears a tricorn hat and that they have hailed him. Thus far he has never answered. But those who were there at the battle, both Confederate and Union, know who haunts the field at Gettysburg.

The Haunting of Valley Forge

He started out of a sound sleep and was almost instantly wide awake. The knock had come on the door, hadn't it? It was time for him to go—no, he was wrong. The knock had not come yet.

Lately he had been having the same nightmare over and over. He would dream that the man had come, that he had answered him and then gone back to sleep, and the next thing he knew there was blood everywhere. All around him men were screaming and crying and dying and they were pointing at him. . . . He couldn't stand it! The cabin was icy cold but he would always wake up bathed in perspiration.

He might as well get up. He shook his head trying to rid himself of the horror of his dream. It was only a dream and he had not overslept. Now, the knock came on the door and a voice called out, "Ho, there! Robert McNairy. Your turn, lad."

The young Scotsman had already swung his legs over the edge of the bed before the last words were spoken. He wrapped the thin blanket from the bed around his waist and pulled his pants up over it. No wonder, for one of his pants legs was almost entirely missing and his uniform was ragged. Hardly a man here at Valley Forge had a whole uniform. They wore rags and pieces of blanket, while bits of carpet took the place of shoe leather.

McNairy was ready to go. He took sentry duty seriously, for the lives of the other men were in his hands. Everyone took his turn and sentry duty was just an hour. But an hour seemed a long time out there on the hillside with the wind swooping down upon him, plundering the warmth from his body.

McNairy stationed himself out on the hillside. His eyes searched out every shadow in the darkness. No slightest sound escaped his ear. Usually all he heard was the bleat of a lamb or the lowing of cows or some other farm animal that General Anthony Wayne had rounded up and driven to Valley Forge himself. McNairy smiled as he thought of the British calling his bold general "Drover Wayne." The troops would have starved that winter if it had not been for this general who cared enough about his men to spend days foraging about the countryside to find food for them.

A few flakes of large, wet snow began to fall. He put out his tongue to taste it. A dog scurried past him, snuffling and tracking some animal. It was a quiet January night and he hoped it would stay that way. There had been enough bloodshed at Germantown to last him for many a day. Would General Howe leave Philadelphia some dark night and attack here at Valley Forge? No one knew, much less the young sentry. He waited and watched and listened.

There was a sudden crunching noise—and this time

There had been enough bloodshed.

it did not sound like a dog or a loose farm animal. McNairy's head strained toward the slight noise and he scarcely breathed. It came again. It was the sound of footsteps and they were steadily approaching. McNairy was surprised, for most of the men were asleep and few cared to visit the sentry on a cold January night.

But from out of the blackness came the figure of a man. The moment McNairy was sure of it he lifted his musket.

"Who goes there?" he called. There was no answer and McNairy's finger tightened on the trigger. He hailed the stranger again and this time an unusual reply came back.

"All right, man. The war's over, you know."

"The war is over?" said McNairy in his soft Scottish burr of an accent.

"Yes, at Yorktown. And Washington elected president. As if you didn't know it, my friend." The figure continued to approach McNairy.

"Halt!" McNairy called out. But the man kept on coming.

"Isn't it a pretty cold night to stand out here joking at the point of an antique musket? We must be close to where General Wayne's men were stationed, aren't we?"

"Yes, and I believe I shall have to take you there, sir."

"Good heavens! Don't you Revolutionary War buffs ever grow up? Out here this time of night playing the fool." McNairy stiffened and held the gun up keeping it aimed.

"Who are you, sir?"

"I'm a history teacher. I decided to leave my motel and take a walk tonight."

"Are you British?"

"No, I'm American."

"You're what?"

"That word is in your history book, man. It means you and I live in the United States of America now. After all, it's been two hundred years since we won the war."

The two stared at each other, and gradually McNairy lowered his musket, for the stranger did not look like a military man or as if he was armed. Blue trousers like skinny pipes came down to his ankles where they flared out. *They needed to flare through his upper legs instead of at the ankles!* He wore a jacket of the same blue with metal buttons and a white wool sweater with a round collar. No breeches, no proper white shirt. McNairy could see nothing of the schoolmaster about him.

"And what of the war here at Valley Forge?" asked McNairy.

"Nothing ever happened here. At least no battle," came the reply.

"I'm going to have to take you to the sergeant of the guard."

"All right. Let's go then. On with your little game." And the stranger began to walk beside him. They were a strange-looking pair—the man in the tattered Revolutionary War uniform and the man in blue jeans.

Sergeant Donald Frazier heard them talking and his face was full of astonishment as he saw them approach. McNairy told him the things the stranger had said and that he claimed to be a schoolmaster.

"You say he knows the future? What kind of prisoner do you have here? And he says the war is over, does he?"

"Of course it's over, and Washington was elected President, then Adams and Jefferson." Frazier looked bewildered. "America goes all the way to the Pacific Ocean now," the stranger continued.

"It does? And what about Valley Forge?"

"Every school child learns about Valley Forge," said the stranger in a friendlier manner.

"I see," said Frazier. Then he recalled that McNairy

was on duty.

"Return to your post immediately," he ordered.

"Why? Nothing is going to happen out here. Howe never attacked Valley Forge," said the prisoner. Frazier looked at him oddly and for a few seconds no one spoke. Then the sergeant turned to the sentry.

"McNairy, I don't know where this fellow came from but I am beginning to think there could be some trouble with him around. Perhaps if the two of you just went back to your post together—I am sure he is on his way somewhere and we might be foolish to detain him."

McNairy began to understand and nod agreement.

As he watched the two walk off together in the moonlight, Sergeant Donald Frazier shook his head. All sorts of crazy things had happened here at Valley Forge. He had

Phantom sentries had been seen.

heard that phantom sentries had been seen out on the hillside and some had seen the ghosts of executed spies. But this man who could predict the future—was he a ghost?

Frazier didn't know. But he never forgot the things the man had told him, nor ceased to wonder when they came true.

Buried Treasure in the Haunted Woods of the Chesapeake

"I was about seventeen when I saw the ghost for the first time," declared Hadgins. "It was late one October night when there was a banging on our front door. It was our near neighbor, Mr. Blough, come over to our farmhouse and asked me to drive to Matthews for a doctor. One of the children was seriously ill."

Several miles from the village of Matthews Courthouse in Virginia and less than a quarter of a mile from Chesapeake Bay is a strange and frightening patch of forest known as the Old House Woods. The woods itself is about sixty acres, and one side of its borders on the bay shore road.

In Revolutionary times an old wooden house stood about halfway along this road in the forest. Although many of the older people in the area declared ghosts had been seen there, Jessie Hadgins, a solid, respected Matthews Courthouse merchant, had a ghostly encounter there that is most vivid.

"I am not apologetic or ashamed to say that I have seen ghosts in that woods and I don't care whether I am

*A strange
and
frightening
patch of
forest.*

believed or not. And what I saw, I saw not once but a
dozen times.

"We had no doctor down here in those days and
when a doctor was needed there was no alternative but
to drive to the village to get him. So, I hitched up our
horse and started to town. The night was windy and promised to storm before many hours. Low-hanging clouds concealed the moon that glowed a dim yellow just above the
horizon. But it was enough light to see by and I whistled
as I drove along.

39

"Nearing the old house I saw a light moving along the road about fifty yards ahead of me in the same direction I was traveling. I had seen lights on the road before at night but they were always a source of comfort and companionship. This one was different. There was something awesome and unearthly about it. The rays seemed to come from nowhere and yet they moved with the bearer or whatever was carrying the light.

"I gained on the nocturnal traveler, and as I stand here before you, what I saw was a big man wearing a suit of armor. Over his shoulder was a gun, the muzzle end of which looked like a fish horn. As he strode—or *floated*—along there was no sound. My horse stopped dead still. I was weak with terror and horror.

"I wasn't twenty feet from the *thing* when it stopped and faced me. At the same instant, the woods, about a

Low-hanging clouds concealed the moon.

hundred feet beyond this creature, became alive with lights and moving forms. Some of them carried guns like the one borne by the *thing* in the road. Others carried shovels of an outlandish type, while others of their company dug furiously near a dead pine tree. As my gaze returned to the shadowy figure, what I saw was not a man in armor but a skeleton, and every bone of it was visible through the armor, as though the armor were made of glass. The skull, which appeared to be illuminated from within, grinned at me horribly. Then, raising aloft his sword, the awful specter started toward me. I pulled on the rein to get my horse turned around but he reared up wildly and I pitched from the carriage seat.

"The last thing I remember is falling to the road. When I came to, it was daylight and my neighbor was bending over me anxiously asking what had happened. Blough said, 'Don't you worry. Your horse and carriage came home without you and that's how we knew to come looking for you.' The best proof of what I had seen was Tom, the horse, who, until his dying day, whenever he approached the woods began to tremble violently and cower. It was pitiful to see such a fine animal become such a victim of terror but the horse must have seen what I saw. This was the first of many encounters I had in that woods."

According to residents of the community, the ghostly skeleton and his companions are Royalists from England who buried a good deal of gold in the woods near the house to keep it safe from Cornwallis's army. Charles II, following the execution of his father by Cromwell, contemplated flight to Virginia and sent chests of money, silverplate, and royal jewels to the colony in preparation for his arrival. The colonists of Virginia were very loyal to the King and Virginia would have been a safe haven for him.

The King's treasure may well have been buried in the haunted woods. Near there a band of renegade pirates ambushed and murdered a group of King Charles's soldiers after they had buried the treasure somewhere on the shores of Chesapeake Bay. The ship that brought the Royalists up the bay and was waiting to return to England sank in a sudden storm and the King was never able to find out what happened to his men or recover the treasure.

But one man saw what happened. Jessie Hadgins stumbled upon them that night in the woods. Hadgins has seen the ghosts of the Englishmen several other times on trips along the bay shore road at night. But Ben Ferrebe, a fisherman who lived along the shore not far from Matthews Courthouse, actually saw the English ship.

"One starry night I was fishing off the mouth of White's Creek out in the bay. It must have been after midnight when, as I turned to bait up a line in the stern of my boat, I saw a full-rigged ship in the bay standing pretty close in. I was quite surprised because full-rigged ships were mighty scarce then. Besides, I knew if she kept on coming, the water wasn't deep enough for her.

"On the ship came, with lights at every masthead and spar. Then I was plumb scared as the ship was heading right for me and would sink me if she didn't change course. I shouted to the sailors leaning forward over her rail, but they paid no heed. Just as I thought she would strike me, the helmsman put her hard aport. It passed so close that I was almost swamped by the wash. She was a beautiful ship but different from any I had ever seen. She made no noise as she passed, but afterward the most beautiful music I ever heard floated back to me.

"Then as I watched in astonishment, the ship sailed right up on the beach and never stopped. Over the sand she swept, floating in the air, and up onto the bay shore road. Her keel was about twenty feet from the ground. It was the only time I saw a ghost ship and I was so scared I wouldn't want to see one again. The ship sailed up the bay shore road to a spot in the Old House Woods and

It was the only time I saw a ghost ship.

then stopped as if she was anchored there. Running down the ship's side into the trees was a rope ladder with men scurrying up and down carrying tools and treasure boxes."

To this day all attempts to dig for the buried treasure of King Charles have met with tragedy. Only the natives who go about their business of fishing or traveling the bay shore road are apparently immune to the mysterious power that guards the treasure. They have seen it while others who have sought the treasure have vanished in the woods, or their empty boats have been found floating in the bay.

Back from the Dead
at Harpers Ferry

It was late at night and near the banks where the Shenandoah and Potomac Rivers meet and embrace that something dank and dark lay stretched upon the chilly ground like a moldering log. The moon rose higher. The *thing* seemed to stir a little—or was it only the October wind ruffling the brown leaves? Then a stronger gust went swishing and whispering through the scrubby growth beside the river. After it had passed, the long, moldering thing began to stir and turn of its own accord. A tall, musty figure—half man, half earth and leaves—rose and walked. *Why can't dead things stay where we put them? Why can't things stay dead?*

Bradley Matthews leaned back, one foot braced against the old building, lifting up his face to catch the breeze off the river. He was home from his job in Washington for a few days. Harpers Ferry was just like it was when he was a boy, only now he had brought his wife and his own boy back with him.

Most of the time he liked living in Washington. He

liked the pace and excitement of a big city. The good jobs and the good money were there if a fellow was willing to work, and he liked work. But every so often he just had to get away and come home. While he was here he would often walk down by the river the way he had done when he was a kid. He would leave the house late at night while his wife and mother talked and he would walk alone and think.

Some places you go back to haven't changed and because you don't have to keep up with all the new buildings and new faces, you have more time for real thinking—about things like, maybe, how far you've come and where you're going. Bradley Matthews had been born into a town like that, where nothing had changed and nothing was ever going to change. Not many places like that these days.

Take this old engine house, for instance. The place is brim full of history. It was first built beside the river, then moved to the top of the hill, and now it was back down by the river where it should have stayed anyway. For hadn't that been where the old man fought, where his sons died, where he almost got himself killed? And he did die later, hung by the neck.

"Not many things worth dying for anymore," Matthews thought, but if he could be sure there were . . . maybe life would be different. Why had the crazy old fellow done it? Come into this quiet little place with his men, thinking he was going to change everything, turn it right side up.

Bam! Bam! The sharp reports of a gun interrupted his thoughts and he jumped halfway up the side of the

Hadn't that been where the old man fought?

engine house. There was no other shelter so he pressed his body against the brick wall and hoped that if there was a fight he wouldn't be seen.

Voices were coming from inside the engine house so he edged along the building to look in the window. He had just reached it when someone spoke up at his elbow.

"Don't you know it's against military law to talk with prisoners?" said a stern voice. Astounded, Matthews turned to find three white men and two black men standing there in the moonlight. The leader appeared to be the tall old man with the full beard and impressive appearance. He was the one who had spoken.

Bradley Matthews didn't like being ordered around.

"I'll talk to anybody I please," he answered.

One of the men whipped out a pistol and pointed it at Matthews's chest, but the old man stretched out his hand and put it on the arm of the fellow pointing the gun.

"Wait a minute, I want to ask him a question. Do you own any slaves?"

"Man, you must be crazy," Matthews started to say, but as he looked deep into the flaming eyes of the bearded leader he changed his mind. The man's clothes were dark and rumpled, covered with leaves and bits of trash but the eyes burned fierce and bright with an intensity that seared him. The old man grasped Matthews's arm and he was terrified.

Bradley Matthews broke and ran. He ran as fast as he could, taking a zigzag course down the brick street and up the hill. He heard the old man shout but he kept running, and behind him came the sharp crack of gunfire and pursuing footsteps. Then an amazing thing happened. A woman he had never seen before ran out from a doorway and placed herself between and his pursuers. He could hear the men close behind him. The woman stretched her arms wide crying out, "Don't shoot him! Don't shoot him, please!"

He didn't wait to see what would happen but fled through an alley, up the hill, and on to his mother's house. He didn't stop until he was in the yard. When he turned to look back down the street there was nothing to be seen. No sound of shots, no shouts broke the stillness. The town of Harpers Ferry seemed fast asleep and the chase had not awakened it.

Back at the engine house a dark figure stood

undecidedly, lifted a musty, leaf-strewn arm as if beckoning others to follow, then headed toward the bluff along the river.

Matthews lay wide awake in the darkness of his bedroom. "Glory, glory halleluia," he thought. "I should have known better than to go down to the engine house tonight, of all nights, for today is October 17th, the anniversary of old John Brown's raid."

"Mine eyes have seen the glory of the coming of the Lord." Bradley Matthews could not get the hymn out of his head. John Brown celebrating? Old John getting up from the ground, of which he was now surely a part, and coming back? Matthews lay awake a long time.

The man's clothes were dark and rumpled.

The Ghost of the Army
of Northern Virginia

The oak trees were covered with their long yellow tassels. That was the last thing he recalled seeing before he fell asleep and the first thing that came into focus as he awoke.

He remembered the day before vividly. He and ten of his men had been standing beside the road to Appomattox Courthouse. They had lost their own guns in the disaster at Sailor's Creek. He had been thinking about how discouraged he felt when his attention was drawn to a Federal gun and caisson drawn by six horses and guarded by several Confederates. The lieutenant recognized General E. P. Alexander and, stepping up to him, he had said, "I've got ten men here ready to serve a gun." In a moment the cannon had been turned over to him and he had posted his men on a small hill overlooking the Appomattox River.

That was yesterday. Now all was quiet. He could see the river, but where had everyone gone? He knew the quiet meant only one thing. The Army of Northern Virginia must be about to surrender. As he started to walk

He had been standing beside the road to Appomattox Courthouse.

toward the courthouse he saw the gun he had used yesterday. It was strange to find it just sitting there abandoned. The surrender must already have taken place.

He went in the courthouse door and inside he was astonished to find a veritable museum. Near him a small boy stood staring at some muskets. There were stacks of guns, a cannon, and Confederate and Union battle flags mounted on the wall. Everything was very still. He and the boy seemed to be all alone. He almost felt as if there were a sheet of invisible glass that kept him from touching the rifles. But it was the cannon he really wanted to

He and the boy seemed to be all alone.

run his hand across, for it was the one he had lost at Sailor's Creek. It was his very own cannon. He had dragged it through the mud at Cold Harbor and he had slept by it many a night. He thought of how he had used the captured Union cannon the day before. And he recalled that final moment of the battle when it seemed that blue-coated cavalrymen were all about his gun crew, slashing fiercely with their sabers. There was a terrible pain in his chest and the memory faded. He clenched his teeth and compressed his lips. What was *his* gun doing here inside the courthouse? To be displayed this way here at the surrender was to almost make a mockery of him. He hurried out into the morning sun but could find no one.

Passing a house, his nostrils twinged with delight at the odor of coffee and the unmistakable fragrance of country ham frying. He was ready to mount the steps and knock on the door when he felt a firm but friendly hand upon his shoulder. He turned to see the first one of his comrades since battle.

"How are you feeling, Lieutenant?" the man asked him. At first glance he thought he knew the soldier. Then he realized it must be a man from one of the other regiments. No matter. It was good just to meet another Confederate officer.

"Better this morning, thank you. I don't know what happened to me yesterday. The battle was a fierce one, wasn't it?"

"Yes, it was. Are you ready to go now?"

"What are our orders?"

"Lee has surrendered. It's all over now, friend. Are you ready to come with me at last?"

He saw the gun he had used yesterday.

Lee has surrendered. Lee has surrendered. Lee has .
. . . His head felt as if it were spinning around and
around. The Confederate officer began to look blurred. He
closed his eyes and leaned heavily against the side of the
house. When he opened them, the man was gone.

He was no longer interested in coffee. He decided to
head toward the tavern for a drink. Yes, that was what
he needed—something to steady him. He opened the tavern door and went in. The place seemed empty, probably
because it was early in the day. Then he saw a man in a
uniform he could not identify and the man was walking
toward him. It was neither a Confederate nor a Union uniform. The man spoke to him.

"Sir, would you like a brochure on Appomattox? The
surrender was April 9th just a hundred years ago today."

The lieutenant held out his hand for the brochure.

"If you don't mind my saying it, sir, I really like that
outfit you've got on. It's authentic-looking, like you slept
in it for a month or something." The lieutenant did not
answer.

Outside, he read the brochure and as he did so he began to feel very faint. Perhaps he should be in a hospital,
or at least let one of the doctors see his wound before trying to find his regiment. Where would the other men be?
All scattered now. Some to the South, some to their mountain homes, and some . . . some dead, dead and gone.
Lucky, that's what they were! He wasn't sure of anything
now and all he really wanted was to be at home himself—
or at least not feel so mixed up, so alone.

There at the foot of the tavern steps he saw the Confederate officer and this time he recognized him. Why, it

was Joshua McKenzie, his commanding officer who was killed at Gettysburg! This was the strangest day, but, thank God, everyone had not left him.

Outside, he read the brochure.

"Are you ready to join the regiment?" asked Josh, and he was. He and Josh, just like it used to be. They would talk this thing over and tonight he would camp with the regiment again.

The Specters of Thalian Hall

What goes on at night in old theaters? Do the ghosts of actors and actresses ever primp before the gold-framed mirrors in the dressing rooms? When the theater is dark and the seats empty, do the rafters ever ring with the cheers and applause of some audience long since in their graves? Mrs. William G. Robertson of Wilmington, North Carolina, would say yes!

Organized in 1788, the Thalians are the oldest little theater group in America. The present Thalian Hall opened in 1858. It boasted a floating balcony so lovely that it was copied by the architect for the Ford Theater in Washington. Most of the famous "stars" of nineteenth-century America played at Thalian Hall, although the Wilmington of that era had only six thousand people and was by no means the bustling city it is today.

Mrs. Robertson has been active with the Thalians for many years, especially during the 1960s.

"I was usually stage manager and I spent many nights at the hall for rehearsals. I had strange sensations in that old theater—often the certainty that others were there as well as ourselves. But, I think it was during *Dial 'M' for*

Murder that things began to happen.

"One evening the cast was right in the midst of re-hearsal, and without knowing why, I began to stare up at the first balcony. When my eyes became more accustomed to the darkness up there, I was gradually able to see three figures sitting in the first row of seats, stage center. There were two men and a lady. I signaled to one of the members of the cast, Chris Fonvielle, and he turned to look up there. In a few seconds Chris walked over and said, 'Do you see two men and a woman in the balcony? I was afraid to take my eyes off them for fear they would van-ish.'

" 'Look at their clothes,' exclaimed Chris. 'They're dressed in Edwardian costumes! Let's go up there.' Chris, his friend Sam Eckhardt, and I were joined by the entire cast, and filled with excitement, we hurried to the balcony. When we reached the front of it there was no one there, although all of us had seen the trio.

"Every seat was turned up save for three. These three seats were right in the stage center of the first row—just where they had seen the two men and the woman sitting only a few minutes before!

"Some of the cast were frightened and very little re-hearsing was done the rest of the evening. But this was not to be the end of it. Several nights later they looked up at the balcony and there were the three ghostly spec-tators staring down at them sitting right where they had been the first night they had seen them.

"I had commented that they looked very much like Fanny Davenport, Richard Mansfield, and Edwin Booth, but it was hard to be sure."

A balcony so lovely that it was copied by the architect for the Ford Theater.

During another rehearsal Mrs. Robertson decided to go to the lobby. Leaving the stage, she started down the center aisle. As she did so, the shadowy figure of a gentleman rose from among the box seats and began to follow a few steps behind her. Unknown to her, her spectral escort followed her to the door of the lobby as the astonished cast watched from the stage. Then the gentleman disappeared.

"She wasn't aware of it at all," said Chris Fonvielle. "I don't know why we didn't call out to her. Probably because we were all too fascinated with watching what was happening."

Mrs. Robertson is equally puzzled by something that

happened backstage during one of the performances of *Dial 'M' for Murder.*

"I was stage manager and was responsible for the wardrobe as well. All the costumes had to be ready for the changes during the play. Sometimes there was only a few minutes from the time the actor left the stage until he must be back on stage in another scene and in a different outfit. One of the actresses had to get into a Victorian dress with dozens of tiny buttons down the front and she had only three minutes to change. Each performance I laid out that dress on a chair and made sure it was ready for her.

"One night I forgot all about the dress and I hurried down to her dressing room just minutes before she was to arrive. There it was, hanging over the back of a chair. Just the right number of buttons had been unbuttoned and the dress was all ready for her to jump into! No one else ever touched the costumes and I was never able to find out how it had happened. I just couldn't believe my eyes when I saw that dress and found that it was all ready.

"You know, I don't think even death keeps some actors and actresses away from this old theater," said Mrs. Robertson. "We have turned the seats up during a rehearsal only to find them turned down again later that same night. Sometimes *they* do not appear for a long time. Then one night they are back again."

And so it goes at Thalian Hall. You can never really be sure who is watching the rehearsals or even sitting a few seats away. But since they are true theater people, does it matter whether they are alive or dead?

Alice Still Walks at the Hermitage

Who was Alice Flagg? What happened to her? And why does she walk on moonlit nights?

Hidden among dense woods along U.S. Highway 17 there is a house where the ghost of a beautiful young girl still walks. It's an old plantation home called the Hermitage at Murrells Inlet just south of Myrtle Beach.

The Hermitage was built in the 1840s. Its magnificent white columns are hand-hewn from giant trees almost five feet in diameter. The steps are bricks brought over as ballast on sailing ships from England to steady the vessels so they would not overturn in a storm. The rooms are large and the ceilings high as in most old houses.

It was late summer of 1849 when Alice Flagg, her brother, Dr. Allard Flagg, and her mother moved into their beautiful new home. A few weeks later Alice went off to school in Charleston for the winter. Her older brother stayed at home to care for his patients and supervise the large farm surrounding the Hermitage.

Alice was very attractive and many young men were interested in her. Some were from families of great wealth and social position but Alice did not choose one of these.

There is a house where the ghost of a beautiful young girl still walks.

Instead she fell in love with a young man who was a merchant, and her brother strongly disapproved. It was his desire that Alice marry a lawyer or doctor or perhaps a young man from one of the old Charleston families who owned huge plantations and grew rice or indigo.

Allard Flagg did everything in his power to discourage the romance but the more he tried, the more determined Alice became. Soon she was wearing his ring quite openly at school although she wore it on a ribbon under her blouse when she returned home for Christmas vacation.

A few months later Alice was the belle of the spring ball in Charleston. Heads turned and the eyes of the chaperons watched while she danced so often with her young

Alice's bedroom at the Hermitage.

merchant that she set tongues wagging. Her eyes were bright and her face flushed and if she seemed to laugh and talk more than usual, no one noticed. They only thought that she seemed very happy.

But on the following day, Alice was stricken with the sickness that was sweeping the area. It was the dreaded typhoid fever. The school notified her brother, Dr. Flagg, who came to get her and take her home. By the time they arrived at the Hermitage her condition was much worse and she was now delirious. The first thing Allard Flagg found on examining her was the ring.

"Alice! You don't know what you are doing, wearing that man's ring," he shouted in anger. Rushing out of the house, Allard Flagg hurled the ring in the river. Too delirious to know what her brother had done with the ring, Alice begged everyone who came to see her during her illness to look for it. She thought about it continually and finally a cousin brought her a ring hoping she would not notice the difference. But, she flung it to the floor sobbing and insisted, "Someone find my ring."

Little could be done for typhoid fever, and within a week Alice died. Since her mother had not had time to get home from the mountains where she was visiting to escape the heat of the South Carolina Low Country, Alice's body was temporarily buried in the yard in front of the Hermitage. When her mother returned, the body was moved to the family plot at All Saints Episcopal Church, where she is still buried.

It is strange that although other members of the family have elaborate markers on their graves, there is only a flat marble slab over the grave of the young girl. Upon her stone is the single word ALICE. Sometimes a vase of flowers appears on her grave. No one knows who brings it. Young people say that if you walk around her grave thirteen times backward and then lie down upon it, you may "talk with her spirit." Others believe that young girls who run around the grave nine times will find that their own rings have disappeared. These may simply be superstitions.

More important is the number of people who have reported seeing the ghost of Alice. They say she is sometimes visible walking under the oaks of the Hermitage dressed in her white ball gown. And visitors in the home

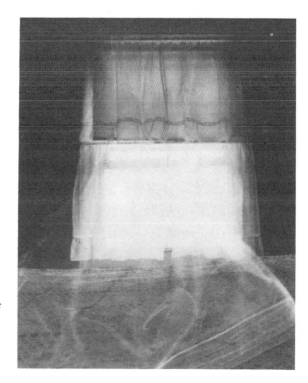

They say she is sometimes visible.

have been startled to see the ghost of a young girl in Alice's bedroom. She is described as wearing the beautiful white dress she wore to the spring ball, the same dress in which she was buried.

Are spirits more restless at some times than at others? There are nights that Alice cannot rest. When the moon is full and the clouds sweep across it, when the mist rises over the fields of the Low Country, when the soft, incessant moan of the dove fills the air, then Alice will walk the ground of the Hermitage that night—looking, looking, always looking for the ring she never found.

The Bell Witch of Tennessee

Beside a highway in Tennessee stands the only historical marker in the United States ever erected to a real witch. Highway markers are not put up until the facts have been thoroughly weighed and investigated. Undoubtedly old Kate Batts would have been very pleased at being so immortalized!

Old Kate haunted what was once the John Bell farm in the beautiful hill country along the Red River. Her cave may still be seen in the cliff above the river although the farmhouse of the unfortunate John Bell is no longer standing.

No one is really sure why the witch haunted John Bell and his family. The first unusual event that Mr. Bell could remember was seeing a monstrous, evil-looking bird staring at him from a fence. He later felt that was probably his first sight of the witch who identified herself as Kate. She would hurl objects through the air, snatch bedclothes off members of the family during the night, hit them about the face, move objects in the house, and insult family members and visitors.

On Sunday, as the family sat in church, they would

hear the witch's voice. Sometimes she would approve of the sermon, but if she did not, she was likely to speak up and contradict the minister. All of her antics were impossible to hide from their neighbors and the entire countryside was soon talking about the antics taking place at the Bell farm.

News of these events soon spread to Nashville where President-elect Andrew Jackson was building his new home, the Hermitage. Jackson and several friends, among them a man who claimed to be an exorcist, decided to pay a visit to the Bell farm and see for themselves.

Jackson and his companions crossed the stone bridge beyond Goodlettsville and proceeded north toward their destination. The party was traveling through the woods and the wagon was rolling along the smooth stretch of road that led up to the Bell home, when suddenly the wagon came to a sharp, jarring halt. The driver cracked his whip and shouted at the team. The horses pulled with all their might but they could not budge the wagon an inch. Jackson called to the men to put their shoulders to the wheel and push. His order was promptly obeyed and while the men pushed, the driver shouted and struck the horses with his whip. The horses pulled and the men pushed, but the wagon refused to move. Time after time the men tried to move the wheels, but nothing happened. Then they decided to take them off and look at the axles. One at a time they examined them and found that each wheel turned easily on its axle. They replaced the wheels and again pushed, but it was still immovable.

Everyone stood around trying to think what could be

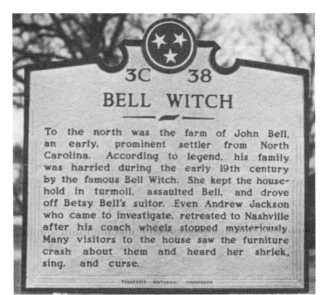

The only historical marker in the United States ever erected to a real witch.

3C 38

BELL WITCH

To the north was the farm of John Bell, an early, prominent settler from North Carolina. According to legend, his family was harried during the early 19th century by the famous Bell Witch. She kept the household in turmoil, assaulted Bell, and drove off Betsy Bell's suitor. Even Andrew Jackson who came to investigate, retreated to Nashville after his coach wheels stopped mysteriously. Many visitors to the house saw the furniture crash about them and heard her shriek, sing, and curse.

TENNESSEE HISTORICAL COMMISSION

wrong. Then Jackson called down from the wagon, "By the Eternal, boys, it's the witch!"

At this there came a wild peal of laughter from the woods at the side of the road and a woman's voice called out, "All right, General, let the wagon move on. I will see you again tonight."

"This is worse than fighting the British," exclaimed Jackson.

The horses unexpectedly started of their own accord and the wagon rolled along the smooth road as easily as before. The professional "witch layer" began now to boast that he was not afraid of Kate, and would run her off himself if she came back that night. The party of men went on to the Bell home and Mr. Bell did everything he could to make his distinguished visitors comfortable.

Jackson was as eager as any of his men to see the witch so they decided to sit in a room by candlelight and wait for her to appear. The witch layer had a big pistol loaded with a silver bullet that he held in his hand as he kept a sharp lookout for Kate. He was a strong, heavily muscled man with a swaggering manner and he brought out the tip of a black cat's tail and told how he shot the cat with a silver bullet while sitting on a bewitched woman's coffin. The men laughed and flattered him while he told his boastful stories until the hour grew late and they became tired of hearing him.

Jackson was restless and began to twist in his chair and yawn. He leaned over and whispered to the man next to him, "Sam, I'll bet that fellow is a real coward. I wish the witch would come, for I would like to see him run."

Andrew Jackson did not have long to wait. For a while all was quiet. The men were tired and no one spoke as they listened for any sound in the silent house. Then it came—prancing, tapping noises like tiny footsteps, and the same strident, mocking voice they had heard from the woods that day rang out.

"All right, Mr. Jackson, I'm ready for business." Before he could answer, the voice spoke to the witch layer.

"Now, Mr. Smarty, here I am. Shoot." The witch layer stroked the black cat's tail, aimed his pistol, and pulled the trigger but it didn't fire.

"Try again," said the witch, laughing. He did, but with the same result.

"Now, you old coward, you hypocrite, you fraud, it's my turn," said the witch. "I'll teach you a lesson!" There was the sound of a great whacking and the witch layer tumbled to the floor. Jumping up quickly he began to dash wildly about the room, running into, and falling over, anyone in his path, like a frightened bull.

"Oh, my nose, my nose, the devil has got me. Oh, lordy, the devil has me by the nose."

The door flew open, although no one had touched it, and out the witch layer ran, yelling with every step. Everyone followed him, thinking the fellow would be killed, but they heard him for a long time as he ran toward

The smooth stretch of road that led up to the Bell home.

Goodlettsville, until his cries finally faded into the night.

Jackson dropped to the ground doubled up with laughter. "I never saw so much fun in my life as watching that fellow get his comeuppance. This beats fighting the British," he declared.

Everyone was startled to hear another voice joining in the laughter. It was the voice of the witch herself. The men fell silent as the witch chortled gleefully. "My, how that stupid fellow did run and beg. He won't come here again to shoot me with his old horse pistol. You can bet on that. I guess that's fun enough for tonight, Mr. Jackson. You can go to bed now."

Jackson looked all about the room while the voice spoke, but although he could tell it was in the room with them, he could see nothing. He could feel the presence of something loathsome, but he was a brave and good man and he did not believe he had anything to fear.

The witch continued speaking. "I will come back tomorrow night and show you another rascal in this crowd," announced old Kate.

Jackson would like to have stayed on but the last words of the witch seemed to make a number of the men uneasy and the next day nothing could keep them at the Bell home, for they had had enough.

Andrew Jackson thanked John Bell for his hospitality and he and his party of friends left—spending that night at Springfield. The following day he was back home at the Hermitage near Nashville with a story he would never forget.

Meanwhile, many well-known people saw the witch's tricks and some who lived near the Bell farm received

You may explore the witch's cave.

frightening visits from her. She continued to harass John Bell until finally she tormented the poor man to death.

If you wish, you may visit the Bell farm today. And if you are very brave you may explore the witch's cave in the bluff above the Red River. Many believe old Kate haunts it today, just as she did in the time of Andrew Jackson. They claim to have heard strange noises and eerie laughter echoing along the passageway. It is best to speak with the owner of the farm before going to the cave even if you wish to enter it alone for it is on private property. At the same time, in the event that you do meet the

Bell witch, you should be sure that someone knows where you are. It would be sad, indeed, to go into the witch's cave and never come out.

The Phantom Riverboats
of the Mississippi

Of all the rivers in America, the Mississippi is the most haunted—haunted by the spirits of the Indians and the French and Spanish explorers. Of the many stories of legends and ghosts, the most mysterious is the one of the phantom riverboats. Somewhere north of Natchez and south of St. Louis they still make their run.

That afternoon had been like lots of other summer afternoons. Jeb was sitting in the woods on the riverbank listening to blue jays fuss and watching the boats as they came down the Mississippi on the way to St. Louis. There were barges towed by tiny tugs, freighters, tankers, houseboats, and every kind of boat you could think of.

He never knew just when someone came up behind him until a man's voice said, "What are you doing here all alone, boy?"

"Just sitting here wondering I guess," replied Jeb. "Wondering why some people have lots of excitin' things happen to 'em and others have no luck at all."

"Like you, you mean?" said the stranger.

"Well, I guess that's what I was sittin' here thinkin'. You know, if I'd had my pick of when to get born I would have said, 'Lord, send me down while those fancy steamboats are goin' back and forth on this old river.' And he'd of said, 'Sure, Jeb, I'll see you get to be captain of one of 'em.' Boy, wouldn't I have won the races though."

"Yeah, they were really somethin', I won many a race myself."

Jeb turned around startled. The riverboats had been gone before his daddy's time. What did this man mean?

"I used to be captain of the finest steamboat that ever sailed this river. 'Packet boats,' most people called 'em." Jeb started to ask him how that could be, but the man went right on talking.

"The boat I remember best was a regular floating palace. I'd stand up on the *Texas* deck and I could see for miles. What a whistle she had, what bells! I just wish you could have seen me steering her eight-foot wheel using my hands and feet at the same time. I knew that river so well I could steer my packet up and down it and never hit a snag or a sandbar.

"One night we were goin' upstream huggin' the bank, tryin' to stay where the easy water is. It was just a little before midnight when I heard a rumblin' sound like the paddle wheel of another boat. The rumblin' from that paddle wheel got louder and louder and when I turned to look, there she was just churnin' the water up. That boat was white and gold with lights all over it. Must have had a hundred windows and you could see inside. There were women in real fancy dresses, all different colors, and you could see men throwin' out gold coins—sure enough *gold*,

"Ever come out here at night, boy?"

I could see them shinin' on the gamblin' table. Cigar smoke was curlin' around the oil lamps. Everybody laughin' and talkin' and the piano playin' like it would never stop this side of the next world.

"I heard the captain's voice yellin' at me to pull over. It made me so mad I hollered back to him that we'd see who moved over first and I got ready to race him. 'Tie down the safety valves,' I called and I could hear him yellin' for more logs to stoke his fires. But we were stokin' ours too. Our valves screamed from the pressure. The sky was a ceilin' of black smoke and sparks flyin' like a million stars as we started to race. Everybody was shoutin' back and forth. Then somethin' happened to one of the boats. There was a terrible boom and, it's funny, I think we won but I don't remember what happened after that."

There was a long silence and for the first time since he had turned around and seen the man, Jeb had a funny, crawly sensation on his scalp, and he hugged his arms close to his body to keep from shivering. He got up to leave, and when he did, the man spoke again.

"Ever come out here at night, boy?"

"No, sir."

"Oh, that's the time to come. Sometimes you can see the boats then. And, if you're real lucky you might get to see 'em race." Jeb looked hard at the stranger when he said that. What was the old man talking about? Riverboats didn't race any more.

"Stoke them fires, boys!" the stranger began to shout along with other instructions that sounded crazy to Jeb. Then he grew silent and, turning, went down the path, disappearing into the gloom and the shadows among the trees. Jeb was pretty scared. Where had the man come from and how did he know so much about the big paddle-wheelers? Why did he say night was the time to watch for them?

When his mother and father were asleep, Jeb slipped quietly out of the house. He could hear distant voices and the muted sound of automobiles. It was almost half past eleven and the point above town where he often went to watch the river was a mile away. Finally, he reached the woods and his feet found the path that led to his hide-away along the riverbank. The moon was blanketed with clouds and the blackness of the forest surrounded him. He wished he had asked his brother to come with him. Then, the moon came out, kindling the path ahead of him. He heard the splash of a fish. There was the river. The moonlight had turned the water into flowing silver and Jeb settled himself where he had a good view. But there were certainly no riverboats, and by now the whole thing seemed silly—getting up and sneaking down here in the middle of the night.

Rumble, rumble, rum–m–m–m–ble came a sound like distant thunder. River and forest were filled with the low roar. It grew closer and louder and Jeb saw a light out on the water. A towboat was coming and the roar was the hum of the big diesel engines. Now the spotlight of the tow flashed bright along the bank near Jeb's hiding place. The tow and barges were so close he could hear the pilot's voice giving orders to the crew through the loudspeaker.

There must have been twenty barges as long as city blocks, dotted with red, green, and yellow lights. With the tow pushing them all together, it looked like a brightly lighted town floating past. Waves sloshed and sucked at the bank. The towboat, with its glittering train of barges, was even more impressive at night than by day, but it was not what he had come to see.

The roaring faded into the distance and once more there were only night sounds. Once Jeb thought he heard a small animal, like a fox or a rabbit, near him. His eyes kept searching the darkness of the river but there was little to be seen. The river was like an old friend, but you never knew how it might act. It could be nice and peaceful or big and swollen with anger, pouring out over the land and reaching into the lower parts of the town.

Jeb's thoughts about the river were suddenly interrupted by the ringing of a bell. It came again loud and clear. If the boy had been tempted to doze, he was certainly wide awake now. He heard the sound of wheels churning along the bank, and out of the blackness he began to see lights and hear men's voices. It could be only one thing—a packet boat!

"Straighten her up, sir. There's another boat close by," called out a man's voice. By now two boats with great paddle wheels pounding the water could be plainly seen. The one closest to Jeb looked like a palace. Her shining white decks towered high above the water and Jeb felt as if he were looking up at a mountain. All the windows were lighted and at each were showy red curtains. Inside he could see glittering chandeliers and men and women dancing. The second story of the boat was the boiler deck and contained a long row of furnaces with fires fiercely blazing.

"Hey, pull over there! S–t–e–a–m–boat comin'," called out someone and the angry reply came, "We'll see who moves over first!" Then there was yelling and cursing. Jeb was able to watch the crew of the boat nearest him. Tall columns of steam were bursting from the escape pipes of both boats and black smoke came tumbling out of the chimneys. As the nearest boat pulled closer he could see some of the crewmen's faces. Where was the captain? He wished he could see which one he was.

"Tie down the safety valves, boys," came the shouted command, and now Jeb saw the captain at last. For a moment he caught his breath, for here was the very man he had seen that afternoon. The stranger in the woods was the captain. Jeb no sooner recognized him than there came a horrendous boom and the captain's boat was covered with flames. Even the river looked like a sheet of fire. Chairs, doors, and other pieces of the boat flew through

The boat looked like a palace.

the air. Crew and passengers, for a split second, might have been limp dolls hurled high by an angry child.

Running, stumbling, falling but getting up to run again until his throat ached and his chest hurt, Jeb finally reached the street to his home. It seemed hours before he could fall asleep. What a terrible sight! How could he ever see such a thing?

More than a month passed and he could not go near

the river. Finally, one December afternoon he could not resist a trip to watch the barges carrying freight from all over the world. Jeb loved to daydream about where they came from and where they would go. He almost forgot about the night he had seen the old packet boats.

Sunset comes early in December and the woods turned shadowy in the fast gathering dusk. Jeb heard the rustle of leaves but did not turn his head. Then the sound came again. Full of dread he wheeled around and behind him stood what he feared most to see—the stranger, the captain of the riverboat. And this time there was a sickening charred odor in the air, a scent of something that had burned.

Jeb shot down the path and out of the woods. He never returned to his secret place along the riverbank again. Did the captain wait for him there on wintry nights? He never knew.

The Blue Lady of New Mexico and Arizona

The sun had set beyond the mountains and the last of the women were drawing water from the stream when Ismene left the pueblo with her jug. She was late beginning her preparations for the evening meal, but since there were only her brother and herself, the meal was a simple one. There would be fish, prickly pears, and corn cakes that Ismene would bake in the ashes of the fire.

As she bent over the bank of the Nueces River letting its icy water flow into her jug, she thought one of the other pueblo women had joined her and she glanced up to greet her. When she saw the woman standing beside her she was greatly astonished. For, rather than wearing a rough cotton shirt and a buffalo skin skirt, this woman wore a dress the color of the October sky and it flowed from about her head down to her feet.

The strange woman's eyes were so kind and her face so lovely that it never occurred to Ismene to be afraid. The lady introduced herself as Maria and she walked back to the pueblo with Ismene, accepting her offer to stay with the young Indian girl and her brother. Despite the unanswered questions Ismene and Ocala had about Maria, the three became warm friends. But if Ocala had not been one of the tribe's most respected warriors, Maria would have met with immediate hostility and probably death, for she was unable to explain how she had appeared so suddenly in the midst of the Jumano tribe.

Daily Maria cared for the sick and the elderly and whenever possible she would tell them about her God. Each day she also found time to gather the children around her, telling them of the birth of the Christ child. When some of the young warriors came near, drawn by her love-liness and animation, she would tell of Christ as a young man confounding the rulers of his day and performing miracles.

Ocala became more and more interested in the beliefs of this young woman and soon he accepted her God as his own. Through him other warriors were influenced and began to believe. The witch doctors watched all of this and, as they saw the people turning to the new God and a religion of love, they became fearful that they would lose their power over the tribe, a power gained through fear.

Angry with Maria they cast a spell over a young girl who loved and followed Maria. She became gravely ill and for a week she was at the point of death. The chief witch doctor announced to the tribe that the girl would die. Maria prayed constantly, for hours at a time. On the seventh day the girl got up, completely recovered.

The hatred of the witch doctors knew no bounds. Their leader secretly gathered around him several warriors who were jealous of Ocala. Working upon this envy he

She saw the woman standing beside her.

easily convinced them that, through Maria, Ocala was growing even more influential. They laid plans to ambush and murder her, knowing that each afternoon it was her habit to walk alone some distance from the pueblo along the banks of the river. They decided to hide where the cot-

tonwoods and underbrush were thickest. Acting with se-
crecy and swiftness, they left the pueblo in the late morning, pretending they were going on a hunt from which
they would return the following day. Ocala suspected nothing, for it was not unusual for a few warriors to occasionally grow restless and go off to hunt, as much to get away
from the daily routine of the village as anything else.

True to her custom, Maria left the pueblo in the early
afternoon. While she was gone, Ocala began to think of
the things she had told him and as he did he became more
and more disturbed. Maria had made it clear she could not
stay long with the tribe. Who would teach them after she
left? Although he had never done so before, he decided
to follow her and talk with her.

Maria had been walking with no real destination in
mind and Ocala found himself catching up with her. She
was now in the middle of a small clearing and he was
about to step out from the brush when he heard the voice
of the witch doctor call Maria's name. Ocala decided not
to reveal his presence. He had long hated the sorcerer and
if Maria should need help it would be best to surprise him.
A moment later he was amazed to see the witch doctor
and three warriors step from among the trees and confront
Maria with drawn bows. Ocala was horrified.

"Shoot! Shoot! or she will escape and cast spells upon
all of us!" shrilled the witch doctor, his face full of hatred. For a moment the warriors hesitated. "Shoot, I tell
you or you will die at the hands of this woman!" Before
Ocala could move to defend her, three arrows sped toward
the helpless figure of Maria. Ocala could not help admir-
ing the composure of this girl. Maria stood motionless. Her

face showed no fear. If anything, there was only bewilderment and, oddly enough, compassion.

The arrows found their mark. The warriors seemed frozen in their places. Not one really wished to go forward, and only the face of the witch doctor was filled with wild elation. Then it began to change and the elation was replaced by fear. Maria pulled out two of the arrows that pierced her body and now she was removing the third from her hip. She walked toward the warriors as if noth-

She was unable to explain how she had appeared.

87

ing had happened. As she approached them they turned and fled.

Ocala rushed out from his hiding place ready to bind her wounds and carry her back to the pueblo in his arms, but Maria stopped him. She showed him her arm beneath the tear in her robe. There was not even a mark upon it! He could not believe it and he was afraid. Maria reassured him and they walked back to the pueblo together. But the end of her visit with the Jumanos was near and as she comforted him she also instructed him.

Nine years later one of the most important men in New Mexico, Father Benavides, stood in front of the Isleta Mission watching while fifty Indians rode across the plains toward him. When they arrived they announced that they had come from a kingdom called Titlas (or Texas), which had not yet been visited by the white man and that they were warriors of the Jumano tribe.

Benavides asked how they knew where to come and they answered, "A lady in blue taught us about Christ and urged us to come here to ask you for a teacher who might live among us." Father Benavides could not believe it. This was one of many remote tribes that no Spanish explorer had visited. He was the more surprised because he had recently received a letter from Spain asking him to "find this lady in blue."

How was it possible for any woman to visit this wild, new country? The explorers were all men. How could she travel alone among hostile Indians without food or companions? Benavides was mystified. For years he questioned and searched for this woman throughout the southwest. Finally, he found her—but not where he expected.

Benavides found the lady in blue not in the New World but in his native land of Spain.

She was Maria Coronel of the Convent of Agreda. Making a special trip there to question her, Benavides found that she could describe New Mexico in detail and knew the names of the Indian tribes and their customs so well that he was convinced she must have lived among them!

Explorers and historians have written about Maria Coronel and the stories the Indians told the first white men about her. None of them could explain how she was able to make her trips to the New World. Some of the wildest tribes carried crosses ahead of them when they greeted the explorers. Maria spoke only Spanish, yet they understood the lady in blue as well as if she spoke their own language.

Is it possible for our thoughts to transport us across thousands of miles to another country? The lady in blue remains a true American mystery.

The Ghost of the Comstock Lode

Some ghosts haunt woods or old houses. But one haunts the darkened tunnels and eerie black spaces of an underground place called the Comstock Lode. He is out of place here—this ghost of a surface miner hundreds of feet below the earth.

From the very beginning of the diggings at th' Comstock Lode in Nevada, odd things happened. This fabulous vein of gold and silver spawned the rough and legendary boom towns of Virginia City, Gold Hill, and Silver City, along with countless bizarre stories.

So many men had been killed in the large mines along the lode that the miners believed the cavernous diggings to be haunted. The passages of the mine were like underground towns with crosscuts and tunnels intersecting every hundred feet. Then there were huge rooms where the ore had been blasted away and hauled to the surface.

Tiny splinters from the timbers that reinforced the mine would catch on fire and the men would be terrified. The fiery splinter would hover over the passage, glowing and burning and then disappear. Sometimes the men would hear the sound of an ax from an unseen hand, and a burn-

The darkened tunnels and eerie black spaces of the Comstock Lode.

ing splinter would split off from the timber and then go out. A few minutes later they would hear the sound of the ax again farther down the tunnel. Aware that gas might ignite and the whole place explode, the miners were full of fear.

Some of the most frightening things began to take place in 1874 when one wintry night the people of Virginia City awoke to see a column of flame sixty feet high shooting up from an old shaft of the Ophir Mine. Men

91

rushed to the spot to put out the fire before the mine timbers could burn and the shaft collapse. But when they reached the edge of the opening and peered down, there were neither flames nor smoke, only a weird light at the bottom of the shaft unlike anything they had ever seen.

The light filled the entire shaft, but this was not all. Down at the seven-hundred-foot level a sound like that of a prospector's pick striking rock could be heard. The men began to argue about who could be in the deserted section of the mine in the middle of the night, but no one was ready to go down and see. Gradually the sound and the eerie light began to fade.

On the first shift at the Ophir Mine the next morning another strange thing happened. The engineer who worked the elevator received a signal to send the "cage" down to the seven-hundred-foot level. He did so and next he got a signal to go one level below, then to bring it back to the surface. But when the elevator arrived, it was empty! No one had worked at the seven-hundred-foot level for many years, as the mine was now much deeper. But the miners reported hearing noises from this level when they passed it in the elevator on their way down to the diggings. They whispered among themselves of hearing a terrible, gurgling laugh that froze the blood.

A young miner named Frank Kennedy bragged that he would go down there and find out what was going on. He took the "cage" to the dreaded seven-hundred-foot level, stepped out, and throwing the light from his lantern before him, he walked along the tunnel. As he expected, it was empty, nor did it appear to have been worked for many years.

Kennedy walked for over a mile exploring the tunnels of the Ophir Mine. He knew the mines were all interconnected and he was afraid that if he were not careful, he might wander into another mine and get lost. With his mind on this possibility he did not hear the faint sound in the tunnel just ahead of him. If he had heard it sooner, he might have turned back, for it was the sound of a

He saw a pale, shadowy figure surrounded by a halo of silvery light.

miner's pick where no miner could possibly be!

Because there were no lights in the tunnel or miners with candles on their caps, it was pitch black behind and ahead of him. Kennedy became very much aware of the blackness but he did not want to go up yet, for the men were waiting for him at the surface and they would think he was fainthearted. He made his way slowly on toward the sound. The pick grew louder and struck with a terrifying regularity. He reached a turn in the tunnel and when he rounded it he saw a pale, shadowy figure surrounded by a halo of silvery light. Frank Kennedy could not believe it when he saw the face. Revolting as it was in death, he recognized it as the face of Henry Comstock himself, the first man to discover the wealth of this mine. There stood the ghost only a few feet away from him.

The phantom that had once been Henry Comstock put down the pick and turned toward him. The face was shocking to see.

The face was shocking to see.

Wrinkled flesh clung to the skull bones in putty-colored

chunks. The eyes were an orangey yellow with pupils that danced as if filled with blue flames. Kennedy began to shake with fear.

"It was January of 1859 when I first dug here. Are you trying to take it away from me? I found this lode, dug the first ore from it, and carted it by ox all the way to California. This mine is worth millions and the gold and silver here belong only to me!" He took another step toward Kennedy, shaking his fist viciously. The young miner stayed no longer but fled back along the tunnel until he reached the elevator. Frank Kennedy was never the same man, nor could he ever be persuaded to reenter the seven-hundred-foot level.

The Ophir Mine was right below the spot where Comstock had first dug and taken his rock samples. Another habit of the ghost was going down the tunnels and one by one blowing out the candles on the sides of the walls until the miners found themselves plunged into darkness. The mine superintendent would come along, and as he watched, the lights would flicker out on one level after another. The superintendent would call out to the miners, "What are you doing here in the dark?" And they would angrily reply, "Waiting for a light! In the devil's name, what trick is this?"

Howling laughter would reverberate down the tunnels and the men would know that the ghost of Comstock was with them again.

Theodosia and the Mysterious Bermuda Triangle

If the wife of a governor vanished it would be a headline story in every modern-day newspaper. This is what happened to the wife of a governor of South Carolina long ago. This particular governor's wife was also the daughter of a Vice-President of the United States.

"It isn't that I want to stay in New York long, but I would enjoy seeing my father for a few weeks," said Theodosia Burr Alston. Governor Alston nodded. He was worried about the long voyage his wife would be taking, but he kept his fears to himself. She would probably have joked about them anyway.

His wife was a lovely, courageous woman. Although still young, she had seen much tragedy. First the duel in which her father, Aaron Burr, had killed Alexander Hamilton, and her father's trial for murder, which followed. Then, the fatal illness of her only son. Young Aaron Alston had died only a few months before, a victim of the malaria so common in the South Carolina Low Country. "Perhaps this visit to her father in New York is what she needs to lift her spirits," thought her husband.

But he still feared for her safety. Those days of 1812 were dangerous ones, for the young country was once more at war with England.

"When do you plan to sail?" Governor Alston asked their dinner guest Timothy Green. "The last week of December," said Green. This young man had been sent down from New York by Aaron Burr to make arrangements for the voyage and take care of Theodosia on the trip. Governor Alston had wanted to charter the ship himself, but to please his wife's father he had allowed Timothy Green to make the arrangements.

The ship Green was to use for the trip to New York was a fast privateer that had been attacking English ships along the coast. But since Theodosia was the wife of the governor of South Carolina, the English had agreed to let the boat travel freely up the coast. The name of the ship was *The Patriot* and it sometimes carried mail from port to port.

Theodosia made preparations to leave as soon as Christmas was over, and the governor asked his uncle, William Alston, if he would escort Theodosia, her doctor, her maid, and Timothy Green to Georgetown harbor where they would board *The Patriot*.

"Don't look so gloomy, my dear," said Theodosia tenderly, when the day came to tell her husband good-bye. "I will be back very soon." But William Alston felt a deep sense of foreboding. First the death of his boy and now the departure of his wife. Standing in front of their beautiful plantation home, he watched the gleaming, black coach with its four white horses disappear down the long shadowy venue of moss-draped oaks. In his heart he did not believe that he would ever see his wife again.

The weather was fair and a gentle breeze filled the sails of *The Patriot* as Theodosia greeted the captain with her most charming smile and allowed him to help her aboard. Captain Overstocks was one of the finest sailing masters on the Atlantic coast.

"How long will our trip take, Captain?" asked Theodosia.

"We should be sailing into New York harbor in less than a week," promised the captain confidently.

"Of course, we may be stopped by some English ships along the way but we have nothing to fear from the British warships since they have already granted permission for our ship to pass."

"And the weather, Captain?"

"Good weather all along the coast," he replied.

Theodosia stood on deck and waved good-bye to friends who had gathered to see her off, and they stood and watched until the first lady's boat became a tiny speck far out in the bay. Little did anyone know that *The Patriot* was headed for the mysterious waters of the Bermuda Triangle.

The sea was calm and the weather sunny as *The Patriot* sailed along off the North Carolina coast. On board *The Patriot* Theodosia talked with Green about her father and her plans for the next few weeks in New York. The doctor retired to his cabin to read, assured by Theodosia that she did not want to be treated like an invalid, a remark she had made often before the trip began.

If we can imagine ourselves as spectators we would probably have seen Theodosia standing watching the cap-

The sea was calm and the weather sunny.

tain, her silky brown hair blowing across her face, her cheeks already turning pink from the sun. Although there was not a strong wind, the sea became a bit choppy as they headed up the coast, and Theodosia braced herself against the side of the boat. She began to look down at the waves.

"The water is rougher and the color of the sea has changed, Captain."

"It may get a bit choppy but it's nothing to worry about," Overstocks replied. He glanced at his compass, frowned, and held it up to study it more carefully.

"Cape Hatteras must be just a few miles to the east of us."

"What is our course?" asked Theodosia.

"We are veering northwest, in fact a little more than I realized," said Overstocks, "but that can be corrected." He turned the wheel and Theodosia felt the vessel begin to turn beneath her. Captain Overstocks checked his compass again. "We still seem to be moving off course. I don't know what the trouble is." He called a member of the crew over to look at the compass. Its needle had begun to spin wildly!

"Assume a bearing due east," instructed the captain.

"I am not sure which way east is, sir."

"What is wrong with you, man?" shouted the captain, who was beginning to grow upset.

"Look at the waves, sir. Instead of coming and going, they seem to encircle the ship. Don't they appear strange to you?"

The captain stared at the seaman for a moment and then gazed out over the water. It was white and foamy and unlike any time he had ever seen it. By now other members of the crew were at the rail and as they checked their compasses and stared at the water, they began to grow excited and fearful. The captain shouted at them angrily reminding them that even if something had gone wrong with the compasses they could always navigate by the sun during the day and the stars by night. But there was no sun visible and the sky was a yellowish color.

Soon the ship began to whirl in a circle. Faster and faster it went, until crew and passengers lost all consciousness. Like a leaf in a tornado, the ship was sucked into the depths of the ocean. As yet unnamed, this was that devilish area later to be known as part of the mysterious Bermuda Triangle.

No one is really sure what happens in the Bermuda Triangle, only that it behaves like some sort of gigantic maw, a place of horror out in the ocean where ships and airplanes disappear never to be heard from again. Often the weather is fine. The ship or plane has reported no trouble but, like *The Patriot*, they vanish without a trace. There is never any wreckage, nor lifeboats, bodies, or calls of distress.

Some thought her to be the ghost.

101

Navy and Air Force planes have disappeared in the Bermuda Triangle, just as completely as Theodosia Alston and her companions on *The Patriot*. What deadly and invisible force does this place in the Atlantic Ocean possess? Is there an invisible doorway that one goes through never to return and tell about it?

On the other hand, perhaps *one* did return. For not long after the disappearance of *The Patriot* there were fishermen who saw the figure of a young woman along the beach of Cape Hatteras on moonlit nights. Some thought her to be the ghost of a poor fisherman's daughter who had died shortly before her marriage. But others say it is the ghost of the beautiful Theodosia waiting for a ship to take her back to her grieving husband. For somewhere out there off Cape Hatteras she drowned and her spirit cannot rest.

Pelican Inn

Pawley's Island, South Carolina: The English housekeeper described it as "a lofty castle. Its builder Plowden C. J. Weston had no idea of the curious reputation his summer home would acquire."

A slave placed a silver tray with a glass of brandy at the elbow of the tall, deeply tanned visitor. The man who sat facing Plowden and Emily Weston wore spats and a button down vest over a dark suit of a more extreme style than most South Carolina planters would consider well-bred. He tilted the glass to his lips before he spoke. Some might have thought him handsome with his bold eyes and wavy black hair streaked with gray, but there was a hard look about his mouth. His name is not a matter of record so we will call him Anthony Bristol.

"I'm surprised you couldn't find a purchaser yourself for your Laurel Hill slaves," he said gazing at Plowden Weston with curiosity. "I heard that Dan Jordan made you an offer for them when he bought the plantation."

Weston stiffened. "No person in the state can have them—not even my best friend. Unless I can find a purchaser to take them away, I will keep them myself."

The slave agent shrugged and drained his glass. "You'll have your buyer before the month is out," said he.

"You make the transaction sound as if you were discussing merchandise, sir," remarked Emily.

"You are quite right, madam," he replied arrogantly. "We are discussing property." Emily Weston flushed.

Rising, their guest placed his empty Waterford crystal glass on the silver tray.

"I hope you will excuse me. I must return to do business in Charleston tonight, Mrs. Weston. Thank you for your hospitality," he said with a deep bow, and she nodded politely.

"You have a magnificent place here," he observed, glancing out the window toward the Waccamaw River. "I marvel at you planters. A plantation here, a plantation there. How many have you left since the sale of Laurel Hill, Mr. Weston?"

"There is Waterford, Hagley, Weehawka, and True Blue—on both banks of the Waccamaw."

"Four. Then I am sure we shall do business again."

Bristol rose taking a few steps with a pronounced limp. Noticing Emily Weston's gaze he responded to the question she was too polite to ask.

"My limp comes from an old injury. A black brute attacked me on one of my early voyages back from Africa while I was captain of a slave ship. I let others do the dirty work for me now."

The Westons accompanied him to the door where Bristol plucked his broad-brimmed, black hat, his cloak

The rear piazza of the Pelican Inn.

with its satin lining, and his gold-handled umbrella off the rack. Then he was gone.

Plowden looked reprovingly at his wife. "Weren't you a bit rude to that man, Emily?"

"Perhaps," she said. "Sometimes I wonder if all of this may come back to haunt us someday. You know that slave saying—something about 'Trouble goin' to fall.'"

"Emily! I'm surprised you pay any attention to that rot."

"Oh, I don't really believe their predictions of doom. It's more that I dislike Bristol's kind."

"Please remember I have to deal with the Hutson Lee Company."

"I wish you didn't. To me, men who deal in slaves reek of what they do."

"Then what about those of us who own them?" her husband asked angrily. "Do we reek, too?" He strode out of the room.

One day in early December of 1859, when Mrs. Weston was inspecting her camellia seedlings beside the Waccamaw River, she was startled to hear the sound of a boat whistle. It was about one o'clock in the afternoon.

Looking up she saw the *Nina*, named after Christopher Columbus's flagship, steaming into view around the bend of the river. Like ebony beads, the faces of the Laurel Hill slaves lined the rails of the boat. Although she was aware her husband had sold them, Emily Weston was somehow still shocked to see the familiar faces of their carriage driver March, the plantation cook Sarah, and the children's nurse Dido.

The slaves from Laurel Hill all began waving and crying out their good-byes to kinfolk and friends while the vessel steamed slowly along. Over a hundred Hagley slaves had gathered along the bank to see them off. It would be a miracle if they ever laid eyes upon any of the slaves from the nearby plantation of Laurel Hill again. Their new home would be on the plantation of a large planter out west. 'Sold down the river' they were on their way to Charleston, and from there they would begin the long journey by water. Plowden Weston's request had been carried out to the letter.

It was a sad farewell. A terrible keening cry rose from the throats of the Hagley slaves, and the slaves on the *Nina* responded with an inconsolable wail. Then, suddenly, their grief spilled over in song, "In case I never see you any more, I hope to meet you on Canaan's happy shore," the words drifting back among the cypress trees even as boat and passengers glided from view.

"Tears filled my eyes as I looked and listened to the wail from those on shore echoed by those on board," Emily Weston wrote in her diary that December night in 1858.

Her husband tried to comfort her with talk of their new summer home at Pawleys. The house was considerably more elegant than the cottages of the other planters. Weston had sent his slave Renty Tucker to England to study architecture, and there were many evidences of his skills. Tucker had constructed the exterior of cypress boards hewn in Hagley Plantation's carpentry shop and transported them by boat to the island. So that they could be easily assembled, he had chiseled Roman numerals into each board with careful hands. Wooden pegs and hand-cut nails held the framework of the house together, and it was underpinned at ground level by graceful arches.

The Weston's new summer home was delightfully cool, for its plaster walls were almost eight inches thick, and an upstairs piazza stretching across the rear captured every breeze from the sea. A boardwalk led from the house through a forest of pine, cedar, and yaupon to the white sand beach. Twenty-foot-high dunes protected the house from hurricanes. On the crest of the dunes stood a romantic, sheltered gazebo.

The Westons found the island an idyllic retreat but their happy years at this house would be brief. The planters society, along with its gracious customs and comfortable lifestyle, was almost at an end. This was the sunset before the long night of the Civil War. From 1862 to 1864, Plowden Weston, although in poor health, served as Lt. Governor of South Carolina. He died of tuberculosis the year the war ended and Emily sold the Pawleys Island property to William St. Julien Mazyck. Over the years the house would have a series of new owners, but somehow it would always bear the mark of the events of the past.

In 1950 it became the home of Mrs. Eileen Weaver and her family. They knew its reputation.

"The house was large and mysterious," says she. "Of course, we had heard there were stories connected with it, but we put no stock in them."

The Weavers named it *Pelican Inn* and continued the Mazyck's custom of renting rooms. Guests enjoyed the inn's spaciousness and good food and its privacy and island setting, and they were soothed by the incessant roar of the surf beyond the barrier dunes.

But almost immediately Mrs. Weaver began to experience the spirits of generations past.

"I was particularly aware of a petite little old lady who would often appear in the kitchen. She would watch while food was being prepared. When pictures were shown to me of people who had formerly lived in the house I was able to identify the lady immediately. It was Mrs. Mazyck who had run the place as a boardinghouse many years ago. Wearing a black and white checked bodice with little fish tails, she would stand beside me and watch me make bread. She didn't make me nervous because her presence seemed a friendly one.

"I am not so sure about something else that happened. It was an eerie occurrence. I was followed about the house and up the stairs by a man with a limp. He would take a step and then he would drag his foot and take another step. I could hear the scrape of his shoe as he dragged his foot behind him. Ducking into one of the rooms I closed the door and while I waited, my heart fluttering, the sounds continued the length of the second floor hall, finally stopping.

"Once I was awakened late at night by the loud barking of our dogs. Going downstairs I found the door to the living room, which I knew I had closed, wide open. There stood a man with a glass in his hand. Leaning against the liquor closet he stared at me arrogantly eyeing me as if to ask, 'What are *you* doing here?' I just stood gaping. My little dog barked and pressed against my legs, and I could feel his body quivering.

"The man wore a rakish looking wide brimmed black hat, a button-down vest, and spats. Strangest of all, when I glanced down, I saw that his feet were an inch or two off the floor. As I stood there he began to move, drifting along through the butler's pantry and into the kitchen.

"Despite his fear my dog followed. He grew bolder trying to nip at the heels that were moving along ahead of him just above the floor. The fellow went through the kitchen door and into the dining room. When I reached it, he had vanished. My dachshund was trembling so that I picked him up, carried him upstairs, and put him on the foot of my bed. Unable to sleep I lay there thinking, 'My God, what was that?'

"When we first moved into the house we made one of the rooms into a bedroom for my daughter, but she kept complaining, 'Mother, I can't sleep in this room. There's too much noise.'

" 'That's rediculous,' I told her. Finally, one night while she was away, I decided to sleep in there myself. I awakened to the clatter of dishes, the clinking of glasses, and voices raised in animated conversation. The tone seemed gay, teasing though very argumentative, and I tried to listen, but no matter how I strained to hear the words, they remained indistinct. My husband and son experienced the same thing, so we moved my daughter's bed, bureau, and chest of drawers into another room and used that one to store furniture.

"Later, after we had learned more about the house, we discovered that her room had once been the old dining room. Perhaps the spirits of slaves who worked there during the Weston's stay sometimes return. I don't know.

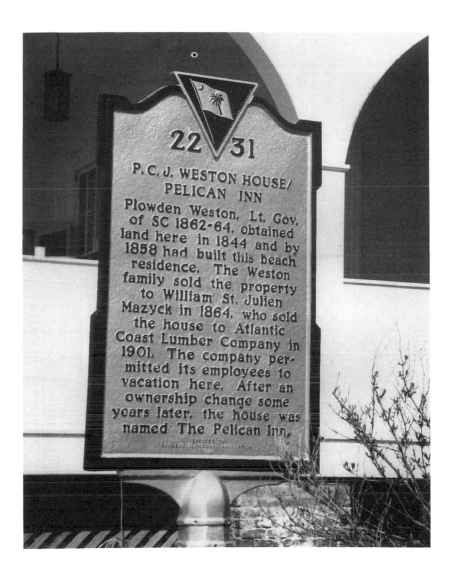

P. C. J. WESTON HOUSE/
PELICAN INN

Plowden Weston, Lt. Gov.
of SC 1862-64, obtained
land here in 1844 and by
1858 had built this beach
residence. The Weston
family sold the property
to William St. Julien
Mazyck in 1864, who sold
the house to Atlantic
Coast Lumber Company in
1901. The company per-
mitted its employees to
vacation here. After an
ownership change some
years later, the house was
named The Pelican Inn.

"Many of the ghost stories have been verified by older guests," added Eileen Weaver.

"You've probably heard the one about the two toy ter-riers frolicking on the beach in front of the Inn. Their mistress used to bring them here long before my time."

Even now, among the sea oats in the tall dunes in front of the Pelican, guests occasionally report seeing two toy terriers chasing each other among the dunes. They are convinced that the terriers are very much alive, but residents of the area know they are not.

One of the best accounts was written by the late Julian Bolick. Author Bolick describes how during the 1890s a proud and solitary lady brought her two little dogs with her each summer. She went on long walks with them. On one occasion their alarmed barking attracted attention, saving a toddler from drowning when the boy wandered out beyond his depth in the water. A few days later one of the dogs ventured out too far and was carried off by a dangerous riptide. His canine campanion found his little friend's body cast up in the foam from the surf. Refusing all food the second terrier grieved himself to death, dying a week after the accident.

In April of 1995 the writer of this story and her husband were sitting in Oliver's Restaurant at Murrells Inlet. In was not a time to talk. It was a time to watch the marsh grass turn molten gold in the late afternoon sunlight. But it was impossible not to overhear the conversation between two couples at the next table especially when we heard the words Pelican Inn. One of the men, who must have been a tourist, said to the other, "You're a native around here. Is there any truth in the ghost stories about the Pelican Inn on Pawleys Island?"

"I don't rightly know but I went over there one day from Garden City to do some electrical repairs," answered the local man. "The supports are so high you can walk around under the house. I was under there when I happened to look over toward one of the brick pillars and saw a hammock moving in the shadows. It was swinging back and forth, back and forth. Not a soul in it! Not a breath of air stirring. Darndest thing I ever saw."

As I thought about what I had overhead, I began to wonder if the spirits of any of the slaves ever returned. The words of the song the slaves once sang echoed in my mind: "In case I never see you any more, I hope to meet you on Canaan's happy shore."

🍎

The account of the supernatural incidents in this story are from a 1983 interview with Mrs. Eileen Weaver who owned Pelican Inn for many years.

The introduction to this story and the conversation is reconstructed. It is based in part upon Plowden C. J. Weston's own statement that he did not wish to see the Laurel Hill slaves remain in the state. It also illustrates the fact that there were merchants in Charleston who bought and sold large numbers of slaves for plantation owners in all the slave-holding states. Hutson Lee was one of those companies.

Information included in the introductory story regarding Weston's proviso that the slaves from Laurel Hill be sold out of state and the emotions expressed in Emily Weston's diary entry is taken from Charles Joyner's book *Down by the Riverside: A South Carolina Slave Community*, copyright 1984, University of Illinois Press.

Angelic Voices

When the town of Conway heard the news that Mary Brookman and Tom Beaty were to be married, congratulations sometimes held a trace of envy. This was a couple who appeared to have it all. She was a highly educated young woman from Maine, and he was a South Carolinian from a well-to-do family. Mary, who loved children, had been employed in Conway as a governess by the Buck family.

"I predict a bright future for that pair," proclaimed Henry Buck. Henry's wife, Fanny, was Tom's first cousin.

At the wedding, the bride's former charges trailed excitedly after her, delighted that their beloved "Miss Mary" would be moving permanently to Conway.

When the Beatys began building a home on Kingston Street, there was gossip in the small town about local craftsmen not being "good enough" and carpenters and mechanics being brought in all the way from Maine. But most residents grudgingly admitted that really skilled labor *was* hard to find in areas closer than Georgetown or Charleston.

When the house was finally completed, there was not

a finer one in Conway. The front of it faced Kingston Street while the back overlooked the moss-draped shore of Kingston Lake. So close was the house to the water that at night you could hear the eerie hooting of owls from the swamp.

The marriage was a happy one. By the winter of 1852 Mary Beaty was busy sewing baby clothes, with the help of her friend and former employer Fanny Buck. In the late spring Mary's mother arrived from Maine to be with her when the baby came.

"It's a lovely little girl," Mrs. Brookman announced

The home that the Beatys built on the shore of Kingston Lake.

proudly, ushering the anxious father in to see the baby afterward. The Beatys named their first born Clara. Clara was followed by Cora, then Fredrica, then May, and finally a son Henry Brookman Beaty, whom they called Brookie. They were healthy, happy children, each possessing different interests.

Clara was always pleading, "Read me a story." Cora sat on her mother's lap at the piano from an early age and began picking out her first notes. Fredrica was a quiet child with a gift for sketching. Plump little May was warm and affectionate with an endearing giggle. Baby Brookie slept most of the time. They were a busy, contented family and for Tom and Mary the days seemed to pass as swiftly as the current in Kingston Lake behind their home.

During the 1850s antagonism between North and South was growing. Tom Beaty, the young Conway newspaper editor, and his New England wife did not always agree.

"It isn't right for the abolitionists in Massachusetts to urge our slaves to murder whites," he sometimes complained.

"I'm sure only a few people are doing that," Mary would say. "We get along quite well in New England without slaves."

"You have your own form of slavery up there," he would retort heatedly. "Children are made to work in your textile mills for twelve hours a day. Is that morally right?"

"That's different," said Mary.

"The real problem is the North has us over a barrel. They charge us an exorbitant price to ship our cotton by rail to their mills. Then they charge us an even higher price to ship it back as cloth. We have to clothe, shelter, and feed the people who grow it. There's no way to make a profit."

"Why are you and Papa arguing, Momma?" Cora sometimes asked after her piano practice.

"We aren't arguing, dear. We were just talking," Mary would say turning back to her mending.

Then personal tragedy struck. The oldest and youngest daughters, seven-year-old Clara and three-year-old May, both contracted typhoid fever. They died within a month of each other. Two merry young voices were stilled forever. "Don't run in the house, girls," Mary remembered often telling Clara and May. Now she would have given anything to hear their running footsteps again.

The Beatys's memorial to Clara and May was a glass-enclosed recumbent statue—poignantly lifelike—of the sisters entwined in each other's arms. After the loss of the two girls Tom and Mary bestowed even more devoted attention on Cora, Fredrica, and Brookie.

In December of 1859 Tom Beaty announced to his wife that he was going to vote for South Carolina's secession from the Union.

"With the election of Mr. Lincoln we have lost our last hope," he told her. "Lincoln is saying the country can no longer exist half slave and half free."

"I think that is true," she responded.

"Well, I believe we have three choices. One is to conform to what the North thinks is right for the people of South Carolina. The second is to secede. And the third is

The memorial to Clara and May.

to die. My newspaper will support secession."

So Tom Beaty became a delegate to the Secession Convention, and his signature was one of those on the Ordinance of Secession. When the Civil War began he served briefly and was forced to return home in 1862 due to poor health. But the Southern cause was dear to him and he set to work recruiting men and gathering supplies to send to Confederate troops. During the last of the War he also served in the South Carolina House of Representatives.

Meanwhile, at sixteen, Cora had become a lovely young girl. Dark haired, with a quick, intelligent mind, she

118

fell in love with Charles Bolton, a newspaperman who worked on her father's paper.

After they were engaged Charles told her parents, "I heard your daughter sing in the church choir one Sunday, and her voice was so lovely I could not resist her." The two were married in 1869. Charles had always thought a honeymoon on a river steamboat would be romantic, and so the couple embarked on a prolonged tour.

But rivers can be treacherous. A few days into the wedding trip the newlyweds heard a scraping sound under the hull. The boat had grounded on a sandbar. While the crew worked to dislodge it, passengers slapped furiously at mosquitoes coming from a nearby swamp. Charles contracted hemorrhagic fever from the bites and a few weeks later he died, leaving his sixteen-year-old bride a widow.

Cora was inconsolable. "I'll never marry again, Mother. Never!"

"Don't say that," protested Mary.

"No. He is the only man I will ever marry . . . for *I shall be dead*. Somehow I know it!" cried Cora, pulling herself from the arms of her shocked mother. She ran to the piano where she struck a series of crashing minor chords that reverberated throughout the house. A cold chill gripped Mary's heart.

During the year that followed, Cora's parents did everything possible to divert her attention away from her grief. They encouraged her to resume her voice and piano lessons, to continue singing in the church choir, and to attend community gatherings.

Although reluctant to admit it, even to herself, Mary

could not forget her daughter's eerie prediction.

On the afternoon of July 2, 1870, Cora sat out in the yard in the swing practicing a patriotic song she was to sing at the celebration on the 4th. Suddenly, she heard terrified shrieks coming from the direction of Kingston Lake, back of the house, where her sister, fourteen-year-old Fredrica, swam under the watchful eye of a young servant. Cora dropped the music and ran toward the sound.

The screams brought the entire household hurrying outside. They saw Cora's music book lying on the ground and hurried in the direction of the screams. When they reached the lake the girls were nowhere to be seen. House servants with stricken faces huddled around Mary. Some stood out on the dock straining to see beneath the swiftly flowing black waters of Kingston Lake. It was as if they thought their imploring gazes could somehow raise the girls to the surface.

"Sister's drowned," burst out Brookie. "Oh, Momma! Momma!" Sobbing, he buried his face in Mary's dress.

"Hush, Brookie! We'll find her," comforted his mother. "Hush, now. You go back to the house with Augusta." She gave his hand to the cook saying, "Take him in, please, Augusta."

"Miss Mary, I'm goin' for Mr. Tom," said Braxton, and the servant ran toward the newspaper office.

Tom Beaty reached the lake shore a few minutes later, breathless. "Were they swimming off the dock here back of the house or from downstream at the sandbar?" he asked. No one knew. But, they all realized that the water was swiftest and deepest just behind the house.

Thrusting aside the brush at the edge of the water,

Tom began to search. Perhaps the girls had been swept by the current toward the bank and been able to grasp a branch. He grew less cautious as he searched and had begun to pull off his shirt to leap into the water when one of his employees restrained him, knowing that Tom Beaty was a poor swimmer.

On the far side of the lake was the edge of the swamp. Beneath its tall trees the area was always the shade of twilight. Had the treacherous current swept the girls along one of its waterways? As the sun began to go down, the shadows upon the lake resembled twisted arms. The men who had been combing the bank went home and returned with boats and lanterns. They would search the edge of the swamp and further downstream.

Tom, who had been up all night, went back to the house about noon the following day. When he saw his wife he shook his head. "No sign of them, Mary." He embraced her.

About mid-afternoon there was a knock at the Beatys's front door. Mary opened it to see an old black woman standing there. "Oh, Miz Beaty," she moaned. "Dem poor, poor girls." Her trembling fingers fluttered up to her mouth. "Ah hates to tell you. De bodies float right up side of de lake near m'ah house."

For the next few days a stream of friends arrived with food and expressions of sympathy.

"I miss the girls so terribly," Mary said to her husband one evening. "Tom, do you ever start to look up with the feeling that Cora or Fredrica is standing by your chair waiting to tell you something?"

"If you mean do I think their ghosts are here . . . no."

"That isn't what I meant. . . Only that . . . sometimes, I believe I sense their presence." He clasped her hand.

Of the Beatys's five children, only one remained—Brookie. More than a year passed. On the night of September 15, 1871, Tom Beaty was working late at the newspaper office writing an editorial. Mary sat in her sitting room mending. She and Brookie were alone.

"It's too hot in here, Mother," said the boy. "I'm going up to bed. Maybe there will be a breeze through my windows."

"Good night, son," she said, and he started up to bed. She assumed that the heat had tired him as it had her. She heard his feet mount the stairs to the second floor. She thought about retiring, too, but decided she would wait for her husband to come home from his office. He might be ready for some tea and cake.

As she sat mending, she was startled to hear strains of exquisite music. It was like a choir of angels, the volume rising in intensity. One lovely voice, hauntingly familiar, stood out from all the rest.

Mary's hands trembled. Her mending fell to the floor. She knew that voice so well; she would recognize it anywhere. It was the voice of Cora, her dead daughter.

"Cora! Cora!" she cried out, rising from her chair. "Why have you come back?"

The answer broke her heart.

"Mother, we have come for Brookie."

Mary ran upstairs. She ran as if she hoped to reach

her young son's bedroom first and bar the door. She would not let them take him! She slammed the door behind her and sat on his bed resting her hand on the boy's forehead, and then she felt his back. The heat of his fever seemed to burn her fingers.

She bathed his forehead and prayed.

"Please . . . please don't take Brookie!" she implored. *"Please,* God."

She pressed her head against his small feverish body. The boy stirred but did not awaken. She sat by his bed until almost daybreak, when she touched his shoulder and realized that Brookie was dead.

That afternoon while Mary and Tom sat at the big desk in the library writing funeral invitations to be deliv-

The Beaty home overlooks Kingston Lake. The black water runs swift and deep.

ered to friends Mary said calmly, "Cora came last night."

Her husband looked at her, his face full of pity. "I'll finish these, Mary. Why don't you rest," he said, rising to put his arm gently around her shoulders.

"No, I'm not imagining it, Tom. Last night I heard the most beautiful choir. It was like the singing of angels." Her husband stood gazing anxiously down at her and she saw the doubt in his eyes.

"Tom, Cora's voice was singing in that choir! I heard it for too many years not to recognize it. And I asked her why she had come."

"Do you mean you saw Cora's ghost?" exclaimed her husband.

"I don't know whether you would call it a ghost, but I know it was Cora and she answered me.

"What did she say?"

"She said, 'Mother, I've come to get Brookie.'"

Tears filled his eyes and Tom was unable to speak. Finally he said, "Then we know that Brookie has been received in heaven with love."

"Yes," Mary replied. "Brookie went in the company of his sister and an angelic choir."

Details of the Beaty family history were graciously provided by Catherine Lewis of Conway, South Carolina. Ms. Lewis, an authority on the history of the area, conducts tours of historic Conway sites. According to Ms. Lewis, Mary Beaty told the story of Cora's coming and the angelic choir to friends for the rest of her life.

About the Author:

With more than twenty books to
her credit, NANCY ROBERTS
continues to delight readers—young
and old—with her ghost stories and
Southern folklore. Ms. Roberts
teaches classes in creative writing
and is a popular speaker and guest
at schools, libraries, and bookstores.
She leads a busy life with her husband Jim Brown in Charlotte,
North Carolina.